Straight Talk

On College

Straight Talk
On College

an employer's perspective

---

100 tips for **success**
in college and beyond

Stephen Young

&
Paragon Press

Library of Congress Catalog Number: 97-92357
ISBN: 0-9659760-0-9

Printed in the United States of America
by Vaughan Printing • Nashville, Tennessee.

SECOND EDITION

In memory of my grandparents

&

Faith and Misch Mischler
Pauline and Darwin Young

STRAIGHT TALK ON COLLEGE
ADVISORY COMMITTEE

Patricia Acklen
Southeast Regional Director, INROADS, Inc.

Dr. Katherine Anderson
Professor, Dept. of Economics and Business Administration
Vanderbilt University

Judith Cline
President, Benchmark Group/Lee Hecht Harrison

Kennon Hampton
Director of Personnel & Recruiting,
Arthur Andersen/Andersen Consulting of Tennessee

Robert Reid
Chairman, President & CEO,
First Union National Bank of Pennsylvania

CONTENTS

FOUR MORE COLLEGE-BASED TIPS
62. Participate in Cooperative Education
63. Participate in Extracurricular Activities
64. Take a Leadership Role
65. Greeks, Etc. - Make Responsible Choices

TIME MANAGEMENT
66. Make "To Do" Lists - One for Each Week and One for Each Day
67. Get a Day Planner and Use It
68. Plan Your Day in a Quiet Place at a Quiet Time

MANAGING MONEY
69. Prepare a Monthly Budget
70. Track Your Monthly Expenses
71. Try the Envelope Method of Expense Management
72. Pay Your Bills On Time, No Matter What
73. Avoid the Credit Card Trap
74. Start Saving Now
75. Pay Yourself First

LIFE-STYLE STUFF
76. Work On Your Weak Points
77. If You Drink, Drink Responsibly
78. Avoid Drugs
79. Serious Relationships - Keep Your Balance
80. Peer Pressure - Keep It in Perspective
81. Take Frequent Walks Outside of the Ivory Tower
82. Practice Random Acts of Kindness
83. Avoid Burn-out

THE JOB INTERVIEW

SOME FINAL THOUGHTS

PREFACE

The key step in preparing to interview students about to graduate from college is the task of reviewing the students' applications. To fill ten time slots for interviewing, I would often have over 100 applications to go through. The decision to put an application in the "yes", "maybe" or "no" pile was made quickly, often in a matter of seconds: a quick glance at the grade point average, review of relevant work experience, leadership roles/participation in extracurricular activities - then on to the next application.

One evening, working late sorting applications, I began to wonder about all of the students whose applications eventually wound up in the "no" piles on recruiters' desks throughout the country. Did these students have any idea when they started college that the actions they would take from day one would eventually come down to a "yes" or a "no" pile?

It is disheartening to turn away an upcoming graduate in search of a promising career. It is my view that entirely too many students wind up being turned away unnecessarily. A student entering college needs to understand that it is not the degree, but rather the strength of the overall college record that matters. With this understanding, if a student has access to information on how to get on track and stay on track right from the start, and the motivation is there, the chances for future success increase dramatically.

Out of this belief, <u>Straight Talk On College</u> was conceived, researched and written. I hope it will be a useful tool in your journey throughout college and into the rest of your life.

ACKNOWLEDGMENTS

I extend my most sincere thanks to my family, friends and colleagues for their encouragement during the writing of <u>Straight Talk On College</u>. In particular, I thank my wife, Debi, for suggesting the "100 tips" format and for her loving support throughout the process, Kennon Hampton and Dave Houser of Arthur Andersen & Company for their many years of guidance, and Pat Acklen of INROADS, Inc. for her enthusiastic support and use of the first edition of this book when it was first "hot of the press".

A book of this nature would not be possible without the wisdom of those with far more experience than I alone have. I thank the members of the Straight Talk On College Advisory Committee for their contributions in the creation and critique of this book.

Last, and most important, I thank the young people who read both the initial draft and first edition of Straight Talk, offering their invaluable insight into what information is most needed and what writing style is most effective.

THE BIG PICTURE

❖   ❖   ❖

1.

FOCUS ON THE PRACTICAL PURPOSE
OF COLLEGE

Do you ever stop to think about why you are going to college? Is it simply the thing you're supposed to do after high school? Was it always a part of the plan your parents made for you? We are told growing up that the purpose of going to college is to achieve many things; to mature into responsible adults, to expand the way we look at the world, to continue our quest for knowledge, even to find a mate! All or some of this may be true for you, but for the vast majority of people, college is a means to a practical end - to prepare for life in the world of work. It's that plain and simple. Most people wouldn't invest thousands of dollars without caring about what kind of return that investment would bring. Virtually all professional careers require that you have a college education prior to being hired. That's the main reason I went to college and I would guess that is the main reason you are going to college. It seems so obvious, but many students don't stop to think about why they are really there. (Believe it or not, it's not just to party!) By keeping the true purpose of college in mind, you will be able to make the right decisions about how you choose to spend your time over the next few years.

2.

MAKE THE SHIFT FROM PASSIVE TO ACTIVE

The changes you face when you begin your college career run much deeper than simply adjusting to living away from home and taking more difficult classes. You have to make a shift from a passive approach to your education to an active one. Here's what I mean by that. You followed a similar pattern from kindergarten all the way through high school. Going to school was not a choice. You were required to get up every morning, adhere to a precise schedule, do your time and go home! I remember that feeling well, particularly during my teenage years.

College couldn't be more different. In every aspect, the choice is yours. What you major in. What classes you take and when. Whether or not you study, do your homework, or even go to class. It's all up to you. No one is going to make you do anything you don't want to do. The choice to even go to college should be solely yours to make. It's wonderful to finally have that kind of freedom, but freedom comes with responsibility attached. If you really want to succeed, you must now take an active role in your education. If you don't do it, no one will. There are, at your college, many seniors with mediocre to poor records that never really took control of their lives. What have they bought with their college education? To put it bluntly, four years of downtime before not being able to find the jobs they're hoping for. This is a tragic waste, both in dollars and, more importantly, in human potential. If you haven't yet made the passive to active shift, now is the time.

3.

MAKE SURE YOUR SCHOOL FEELS RIGHT

People choose the colleges they go to for lots of different reasons. Reputation, location, size, and family history are among the factors that often go into the decision-making process. Sometimes, though, no matter how carefully you research and study your options, you can find yourself at a school that is simply not meeting your needs. Whether academic, extracurricular, social or environmental, if a school doesn't feel right, you are not likely to perform well there. Should you find yourself in this predicament, discuss your concerns with your family and/or anyone whose advice you trust. If the answer is that you need to make a change, you have a few options. You may elect to finish out your term or school year, then seek out another school over the summer. You may decide to withdraw immediately, if you're at the beginning of a term and your record will not be affected, and begin a new college search right away. Another plan of action other than these prior examples may be best for you. What matters is taking action to place yourself in a new college setting where you can excel. As you will learn as you read on, your college record is the key to your future. Therefore, you must find the learning environment that is best for you.

4.

SET AND MANAGE YOUR PRIORITIES

Over the long haul and day to day, all of us must set and manage priorities. Put simply, there's always a lot more stuff to do in a given period of time than can possibly be done. Therefore each part of all that "stuff" has to be ranked in order of importance; i.e. priorities must be set. Managing your priorities involves the never-ending process of reassigning each task's rank as compared with all of the other tasks to be done. Then you can set about each task in order of importance. You probably have already discovered that this isn't as easy as it sounds! It's often difficult to decide what's more important than what. Well, I hate to tell you this, but it's even worse in the working world! The good news is the more you learn about setting and managing priorities in college, the better equipped you'll be to excel in your new career.

Here are a few things to think about: First, accept the fact that you can't do it all. No one can. Second, once you've accepted this, make a point to at least try to get to the most important things. Third, sometimes it's tough to learn what's the most important thing. It takes time. Pay attention to those people whose priority-setting skills you admire and learn from them. Last, once you've set your priorities the best you can, let the stress go and focus on accomplishing each task one by one. As the old saying goes, "How do you eat an elephant? One bite at a time!"

5.

KEEP THE SEE-SAW OFF THE GROUND

This is the visual model I use to describe maintaining a balanced life. With so much emphasis placed on academic performance, students often forget that it's important to develop other qualities. Making time to participate in extracurricular activities, getting some real-world work experience and just simply having fun are vital to becoming a well-rounded, healthy individual. The see-saw makes a good analogy because it's important to understand that the see-saw doesn't have to be perfectly level. If you're one of those rare people able to place an equal amount of emphasis between academics and other activities, that's great.

However, if you happen to place more emphasis on one over the other, that's fine too. The key is to have enough of both to keep the see-saw off the ground. Get the picture?

6.

DON'T GET PUSHED AROUND

It's normal to feel insignificant on a college campus. Sometimes you can find yourself completely lost in the crowd - especially at larger universities. When this happens, it's easy to feel overpowered by "the system," just another student trying to work your way through the maze as best you can. Sound familiar? Listen! Don't let your college years pass you by that way. Sometimes the system is like a maze, but you don't have to get lost in it. You can rise above it all when you see the maze for what it is. Believe me, it's a lot easier to work with the system from that perspective than to just passively take what the system dishes out.

Remember, it's your money and you're purchasing something tangible. You are purchasing an education for yourself. You should expect to get your money's worth! Don't settle for anything less.

7.

NEVER FORGET THAT YOU ARE THE CUSTOMER

It sounds a bit cold-hearted, but the bottom line is that a college is a business. A college has to make money or at least break even, like any other business. It has employees (professors, service workers, etc.), produces products (graduates, research, etc.) and, most definitely has customers - students and former students, corporations and governments. There's upper level management - the president, vice presidents, deans, etc.; a marketing team - the recruiting office, development office; you get the idea.

Now, pretend for a moment that instead of buying a year of college you decided to buy a car. How would you feel if, after driving the car off the lot, it didn't perform as expected? What would you do? Is your college education all that different? Do you think of your education as a product you are buying? For the money you are spending, you should! Keep in mind that, as the customer, you must do your part. It's not fair to complain to the car dealer if you forgot to put oil in your car. In the same way, you have to apply yourself to learn as much as you can. However, at the same time, your college owes you a top-quality educational experience, from the content of its course offerings, to the ability of its professors to teach, to the safety of its dormitories, and effectiveness of all other student services. Don't ever forget that you are the customer. If at any time you feel that you are not receiving the level of service you are paying for, make your feelings known immediately. Your college is there to serve you, as long as you do your part.

8.

TO THINE OWN SELF BE TRUE

This famous line rings true in so many ways in life, and certainly applies to the college experience. Before you go any further with your college education, ask yourself a really tough question. Are you preparing for what you want to do in life, rather than preparing for what you think you ought to do or what someone else wants you to do? If your answer is honestly a "no", put on the brakes and re-group. Life is short. It's not worth spending your life in a career that you will not enjoy, no matter how much it pays, what social status it conveys or how highly others will think of you. Only you know what makes you happy. If that means you need to make a change, do it now, before you spend thousands of dollars preparing for an empty career. Now, keep in mind that no endeavor is fun all of the time. Even the most loved vocations have their not so enjoyable periods. Use the "most of time" test. If what you are preparing for career-wise will bring you enjoyment most of the time, you're in good shape. If not, you need to make a change.

Note: If you aren't sure of what you want to do with your life yet, don't worry. Focus on completing a solid base of course work your first two years, and obtain career counseling from your guidance center in order to find a direction by the end of your sophomore year.

ACADEMICS

9.

EVERY YEAR COUNTS - VERSION ONE

There is no concept in this book that I want you to understand more than this one. Let's walk through this together. What's the practical purpose for going to college? That's right. To prepare for a career in the working world. How do you start that career? By interviewing for an entry-level position prior to graduation. How do you get such an interview? Typically by submitting an application and/or resume to your companies of interest via your college placement office. Here's what happens then: a corporate recruiter will review all of the applications forwarded from your college's placement office, picking out the applications of the students he or she would like to interview. It's important to note that an interviewer does not usually interview all of the students who submit applications. In the case of the firm that I recruited for, we would usually interview about 10% of the students who sent in applications. How did we decide which students to interview? By looking at each student's overall record as shown on his or her application. Why should any of this matter to you now? Because your academic performance, which is a key criteria evaluated, is an average of all of your course grades over your *entire college career*.

10.

EVERY YEAR COUNTS - VERSION TWO

Let me explain this concept another way just to make sure it sinks in: what you do academically as a freshman and sophomore matters just as much as what you do as a junior and a senior. The reason is that prospective employers look at your average overall performance.

One of the biggest myths I consistently hear is that it is okay to "blow off" your freshman year and take your time getting adjusted to college life. This is simply not true. Recruiters pass over countless applications of students who have done just that.

Keep in mind that the recruiter has no way of knowing why your academic average is low, and unfortunately, doesn't have time to care. The moral to this story: you have to get on track quickly and stay on track to position yourself for those great career opportunities.

11.

YOUR GPA - IT CARRIES A LOT OF WEIGHT

Your grade point average (GPA) is the standard measure of academic accomplishment and is one of the most important pieces of information recorded on a job application or resume. The competition for the best jobs is intense. Employers will use your GPA as a key benchmark in judging your academic performance against other candidates. While having a strong GPA is no guarantee that you will land the job you want, a weak GPA can knock you out of the running right from the start. Therefore, focusing on having the highest possible GPA should be one of your most important objectives in college.

12.

YOUR GPA -
IT DOESN'T SAY WHAT YOU THINK IT DOES

❖ ✎ ❖

A common myth about a GPA is that employers look to it as an indication of intelligence. This is not true. Many highly intelligent students have lower GPAs than students of average intelligence. It is this very fact that sheds light on why employers do think the GPA is important. The GPA is important because it provides an indication of dedication to success and willingness to work hard, both very desirable traits in an employee. Remember, the GPA is one of the few consistently available pieces of information that employers have in their evaluation process. An interviewer won't have the chance to really get to know you during a job interview. Never forget that to a potential employer, your GPA is a measure of your level of dedication to success and your willingness to work hard.

13.

TEST SCORES - THE BUILDING BLOCKS OF THE GPA

In most cases, your test scores determine your overall grade in any course; subsequently, all of these course grades are averaged together to determine your GPA. Therefore, a specific objective of yours should be to make the highest test scores you possibly can. That sounds fairly obvious and straight-forward. Just study until you know the subject matter backwards and forwards and you're bound to do well, right? Not necessarily! An in-depth knowledge of the subject matter is a great goal, but there is more to it than that. You have to learn how to prepare for and how to take tests.   This is a skill unto itself that is above and beyond the particular subject matter you are being tested on. Mastering the "How To's" of test preparation and test taking is the key.

14.

THE MORE TIME YOU PUT INTO A STUDY SESSION, THE MORE INFORMATION YOU'LL RETAIN --- NOT!

❖ ✎ ❖

It is amazing how many people believe that length of study time determines how much is learned. Unfortunately, many students waste valuable time studying too long when they could be spending it doing other things that might be a lot more fun! Let me explain.

A graph of the information your brain absorbs versus the time spent during a study session would look something like this:

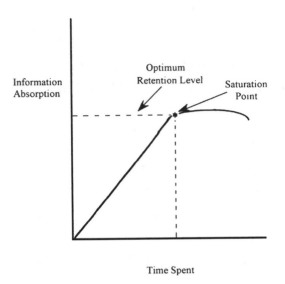

Time Spent

During the first phase of your study time your brain readily absorbs information, but its ability to retain information reaches a limit, then rapidly decreases the longer you study. Continuing to study past this "saturation point" can actually become counter-productive.

Determining your optimum retention level is something you will have to figure out for yourself. During your study time, take note of when you begin to feel peaked out. Fatigue and a decreased comprehension level are two signs that you've been at it too long. When you reach this point, you might as well take a break or quit.

15.

SHORT-TERM AND LONG-TERM MEMORY

Your brain's ability to store and subsequently retrieve information is a process called memory. There are two types of memory capacity; short-term and long-term. With short-term memory, the brain readily absorbs information, but can only retain it for a limited amount of time. Long-term memory is just the opposite. Information is not absorbed as readily, but is retained longer. Now look back at the graph we just reviewed -- as far as memory is concerned, everything the graph shows is related to short-term memory.

Taking a test utilizing only short-term memory is a dangerous proposition. You may not remember everything needed. However, if you study up to your optimum retention level (see graph) over regularly spaced intervals, much of the information you take in will be committed to long-term memory. This is when true learning occurs, and your test grades will reflect this.

16.

IF YOU HAVE A GOOD UNDERSTANDING OF THE SUBJECT MATTER, YOU'LL DO WELL ON THE TEST -- NOT NECESSARILY!

Having the knowledge in your head is no guarantee that it is going to magically appear on your test paper. And let's face it, if what appears on your test paper isn't what the professor expects to see, then whether or not you have the knowledge makes absolutely no difference. I know that seems unfair, but it's reality. Remember, knowledge itself doesn't get the job done. It's the application of knowledge that's important. A test is the professor's way of determining that you know how to apply the knowledge you have in a practical and tangible way. Our upcoming points will cover various ways you can best prepare to do well when it really matters - on the test.

17.

AVOID PULLING ALL-NIGHTERS

All-nighters, or any other type of marathon study sessions are very inefficient and ineffective ways to study. Now don't get me wrong - if you have a test tomorrow, and you haven't studied the material at all, a cram session is certainly better than nothing. But that's not the point! You need to *plan ahead* to avoid this situation in the first place - something we'll discuss more later in the book. You will find that you will perform best by studying up to your optimum retention level over the course of multiple study sessions. Remember why? That's right. Because only then will the information you are studying be committed to long-term memory.

18.

TAKE NOTES ACTIVELY

This may be one of the most practical tips in this book for two reasons. First, no one ever tells a new college student how to take notes. Often, students have had no need to take notes in high school and they come into college "winging it." Second, many college seniors are horrible note-takers, which indicates "winging it" isn't the best way to learn!

Note-taking should be an active, rather than passive activity. It requires thought throughout the process. Many students are passive note-takers, acting as little more than stenographers. They just sit there, taking dictation, trying to write down everything they hear. This is a very inefficient and ineffective way to take notes.

A good note-taker is always analyzing - looking behind the scenes - trying to see what the professor is really talking about. Key ideas are written down, not every word. Your brain should act as a filter, taking in the relevant points and discarding the rest.

Remember, a professor's lecture provides valuable insight to what that professor finds important and what her expectations of you will be on tests. By taking short, concise notes, you will have the key information needed when you begin test preparation.

19.

AVOID PLAYING MENTAL LEAP-FROG

One of the most common note-taking problems comes from playing "mental leap-frog". This happens when you get so caught up in writing that you don't hear what the professor says next. Before you know it, you'll have a page of notes that only contains half of the relevant points! I found that I did this time and time again during my freshman year, and apparently, so did my classmates! It sometimes took three or four of us to piece together one complete set of notes from each of our efforts. Fear not, as we discussed in the previous point, there is a cure for this debilitating dilemma. By writing down the relevant points in a short and concise manner, and filtering out the fluff, you'll find that you will no longer miss a thing. Keep in mind that you won't develop good note-taking skills overnight. Like anything else, becoming a good note-taker takes practice, practice, practice.

20.

GO TO CLASS

A professor at one of our country's top universities shared something surprising with me. The main concern she and her colleagues have is that many students, particularly freshmen, don't show up for class! This puzzled me at first. Why would anyone spend thousands of dollars for an education, then not even go to class? I think part of the reason has to do with that feeling of new-found freedom you get when you first get to college. For some, that freedom translates into "what can I get away with today?". Cutting class may give you a sense of that power, of being able to do or not do whatever you feel like. If you're one of those class cutters out there, I hope you have figured out by now that you're not doing yourself any favors. None of the advice in this book will matter much if you don't make it to the starting line! Want to feel really powerful? Start knocking down good grades in tough classes. Step one: show up for class.

STUDY METHODS

There are many ways to study, and which one or ones you use will depend a lot upon your individual style. The following methods are tried and true, road-tested. You should give them a try if you haven't yet hit upon a way to study that works for you. At least one of them might fit you just right.

21.

REREAD THE COURSE MATERIAL

❖　📖　❖

This method and the following method are based on the premise that if you repeat something enough times, it will finally sink in. While I am not convinced that this is the most efficient way to study, there is no question that for many, rereading your text and other assigned materials works. To make this method truly effective, make sure that you are really letting the points hit home and make sense. Just reading words with no comprehension is a complete waste of time. If, after one or two tries, rereading isn't helping your comprehension level, seek help from the instructor or a fellow classmate.

22.

COPY OVER YOUR NOTES

❖　📖　❖

Recopying your notes works on the same premise as rereading the course material. The students I have encountered that swear by this method of studying indicate that recopying their notes gives them an opportunity to really understand what the instructor discussed in class without the pressure of trying to get everything down on paper. Employing our previous note-taking advice may eliminate the need for this study method. Regardless, you should give this method a try a few times and compare it with the other methods listed in order to evaluate it fairly.

23.

REWORK YOUR HOMEWORK PROBLEMS

❖ 📖 ❖

Reworking your homework problems is most effective when you do so without any crutches. Don't look at your notes or back at the text while working. Instead, focus on remembering how the instructor worked similar problems in class. After giving it your best shot, pick up your crutches and see how you did, taking special care to isolate where you went wrong and why.

24.

FIND A STUDY PARTNER

❖   📖   ❖

Studying alone works well for some, but for others, studying in pairs or groups is much more effective. If you're one of those people, seek out a study partner for each course. If possible, find someone whose style is a bit different from your own. Each of you will have different insights regarding the course material that you can share, giving both of you a better overall understanding. When memorization of facts or formulas is required, drilling each other using flash cards or fill-in-the-blank questions is extremely helpful. The greatest downfall to this method is the tendency to get off track and talk about things more interesting than the work at hand. In order to be most effective, establish ground rules up front and stick to them whenever you get together.

25.

FORM A STUDY GROUP

❖   📖   ❖

Group study can be particularly effective for certain types of courses. As with an individual study partner, a good study group can bring a variety of strengths to the table. This type of study is most effective for courses in which discussion question tests are given. By discussing each issue to be tested in a group setting, multiple viewpoints will arise, adding both depth and breadth to each answer. Each person in the group should make notes during the discussion. Later, working alone, each member should review his or her notes, drafting mock answers that reflect the individual's style.

MY FAVORITE STUDY METHOD

26.

PRACTICE WHAT YOU TAKE - THE CONCEPT

❖　📖　❖

"Practice what you take. " This simple phrase describes the fundamental principle behind the study method I used to prepare for tests when I was in college. Think about it. To do well at any activity requires practice. To excel at a sport or to become proficient on a musical instrument requires practice, practice, practice. Why should developing test-taking skills be any different? Certainly the study methods described previously have value - you may personally swear by one or more of them. However, for me, nothing proved more effective than practicing taking the test ahead of time.

To be honest, this was something I really learned by accident. Every time I practiced taking a test beforehand, I always made a better grade than when I didn't. And what was even better was that this method worked in every class I took.

27

PRACTICE WHAT YOU TAKE - WHY IT WORKS

❖ 📖 ❖

Pretend you are a brain. No, I'm not talking about being a whiz-kid; I mean pretend you are an actual brain! Think about what you have to cope with during a test. First, let's face it, taking a test is a stress-inducing experience. Try as you may to make the rest of your body relax, the desire to perform well causes you to stress out - big time. You're so busy trying to deal with the stress, you lose track of where you put all of that information that the test is asking for. And that, my friends, is what happens when you freeze and go blank during a test. Has that ever happened to you? Me too. Definitely not fun.

On top of it all, the process of taking the information in your head and structuring it into the desired format for application on a test requires a significant part of your brain's resources. And these are resources that aren't being used to retrieve additional information.

When you practice taking a test ahead of time, you allow your brain to spend more time retrieving information and less time figuring out how to structure it during the actual test session when stress levels are high. Oh, and there's one more side benefit. Since you practiced taking the test, the actual test will look more familiar and your overall stress level will go down, freeing up even more of your brain's resources.

28

PRACTICE SHOW-YOUR-WORK PROBLEMS
THE MOST

❖ 📖 ❖

Some tests are more difficult to take than others. True/false, multiple choice and fill-in-the-blank test structures are generally very easy to practice because these styles are very basic and easily reproducible. Show-your-work tests require much more analysis. This is because multiple elements exist within each question that reflect a professor's style and expectations. Practicing taking show-your-work tests are essential in my view. It is in these types of tests that professors expect to see their approach to problem-solving reproduced on the test paper. Now, I know what you're thinking. They should want to see your approach problem-solving, not theirs. In some rare cases, this may be true. However, consciously or unconsciously, most of the time, instructors want to see their approach validated, and when they do, you will score high. (You will find that this makes a good model for dealing with others in general, but that's another book!)

DEVELOPING PRACTICE TESTS

29.

USE PREVIOUSLY-GIVEN TESTS AS A MODEL

❖ 📖 ❖

Professors may be eccentric at times, but they are usually very consistent from class to class and from year to year. Therefore, working through a professor's old tests is an excellent way to practice for an upcoming test. Many college and university libraries keep copies of professors' previously given tests on file. See if yours does. If not, find out if your professor will allow you to copy old tests from his personal files. (No, I'm not kidding - many professors are happy to share old tests with you.)

30.

SEEK OUT SOMEONE WHO HAS BEEN
PREVIOUSLY TAUGHT BY THE PROFESSOR

❖ 📖 ❖

Fellow students who have previously had the same professor in the same class that you are taking can be of great help to you. Many will have kept copies of their old tests, should you need another source. Even better, these students will also be able to shed light on the professor's personality, teaching methods and basic expectations. Don't overlook the valuable advice they can give you.

31.

PAY ATTENTION IN CLASS

❖ 📖 ❖

That sounds pretty obvious, doesn't it? Well it's not as obvious as you may think. While most people pay attention in class to what is being presented, very few people pay attention to how it's being presented! That's just as important. Watching and listening to how the professor presents information in class provides valuable insight into what that professor's expectations of you will be when you have to provide that information back to him on a test.

Hint: pay very close attention to what the professor writes on the board. Believe it or not, colleges actually send professors to classes on how to be better teachers, and one of the key things these classes emphasize is to always write on the board the key points students are expected to know. Now, I know what you're thinking. There's a lot of profs out there who obviously didn't pay attention in that class! True enough. Nevertheless, many do use this method, so pay attention and watch the board.

32.

LEARN FROM EACH TEST GIVEN

❖ 📖 ❖

You may not be fortunate enough to have been able to obtain copies of old tests for a given professor. This doesn't mean you have to stay in the dark forever. You can quickly get on the right track as soon as the first test has been given. By and large, professors are very predictable, and while subsequent tests will certainly cover different material, the structure of the tests will probably remain exactly the same. Studying the structure of the first test, coupled with information presented in class and in the text, will enable you to create your own sample test prior to each actual test.

33.

LOOK FOR TRENDS IN THE TYPE
OF HOMEWORK PROBLEMS ASSIGNED

❖ 📖 ❖

Most professors will assign homework problems that are very similar to the type of questions they will give you on the test. When this is the case, simply reworking your homework problems (see #23) prior to a test is, in effect, practicing taking the test. Of course, there are professors who will assign many different kinds of problems for homework. If this is the case for you, place emphasis on the previous point discussed and pay attention to which type of homework problems the professor tends to rework in class. They will usually be of the same structure as those that will appear on the test.

THE STUDY ROUTINE

34

DEVELOP YOUR STUDY ROUTINE

❖ 📖 ❖

The key to any good study routine is based around two simple concepts - organization and consistency. No matter what study methods you employ, you will learn more, retain more and perform better on tests if you approach studying in an organized and consistent manner. Once you have developed a system that works for you, there will be only one thing left to do: stick to it! Make sure you go about studying the same way every time. This will seem hard at first, even tedious. But before you know it, you will get into a habit. Once studying becomes a habit, it will also become second nature, and the organization and consistency required to study effectively will happen automatically.

This may seem like a strange comparison, but if you think about it, it's really not too much different from learning to wear a seat belt. I don't know about you, but I used to hate to wear my seat belt, but, realizing it would probably save my life one day, I stuck with it. Over time, it's become second nature to me. That is how studying will become for you if you will develop your own routine and stick to it! You know, the seat belt comparison isn't so strange after all. Turning your study routine into a habit will one day "save your life" in more ways than you can imagine.

A PROVEN STUDY ROUTINE
TO USE AS A GUIDE

(#35 - #46)

35.

GATHER YOUR MATERIALS

❖ 📖 ❖

Never begin a study session in a particular subject without having all of the components around you that relate to that particular subject. If you are using a textbook, make sure you have it. Make sure you have all of your class notes, all past homework that you have worked, any sample test questions you may have gathered, and anything else you can think of that may come in handy. Nothing will get you off track quicker in your study session than breaking your train of thought to stop and look for something that you need in order to continue.

36.

FOCUS ON WHAT YOU ARE DOING

❖ 📖 ❖

I can't stress this enough. Distractions are deadly when it comes to studying and retaining information. Learning to put everything out of your mind except the subject you are studying is not easy. It takes practice, but it is essential. The key word here is focus. If the environment that you are currently studying in does not allow you to focus, change environments! If your dorm is too noisy, go to the library. If the library is too quiet, find your own spot! The key is to find a place where you are comfortable and where you can focus. A side note: different people have very different ways of focusing. My college roommate, who is my best friend to this day, could only study calculus with headphones on playing loud music! How is that possible, you ask? I have no idea! The bottom line is, strange or not, he created an environment where he could focus.

37.

READ OVER YOUR NOTES AND SKIM THE TEXT

❖　📖　❖

It is always helpful to read over your notes and perhaps recopy them. If you don't feel that your notes are enough, then you also need to skim the text. Note that I said skim the text, not read the entire text. If you are taking several classes where reading assignments are given from the text, you will wind up with more assigned than you could ever get to, even if you read 24 hours a day! Unfortunately, many students start out trying to accomplish this impossible task and only read a small part of the way before they get frustrated and quit. It makes much more sense to spend your time reading over your notes and skimming the text, picking up key phrases, first sentences of paragraphs, formulas and anything else that sticks out. Use a highlighter, or underline items.

Hint: you may also want to jot this key information down on a single sheet of paper, perhaps one per chapter, to save time later when studying for finals.

38.

DO YOUR HOMEWORK - BUT USE COMMON SENSE

❖ 📖 ❖

Unless you are required to turn in your homework assignments as part of a grade in your class, only work problems with a structure like those that will be on the test. Let me say it another way: don't waste your time with homework problems that aren't like those that will be on the upcoming test. You will not be surprised to learn that every educator who has proofed this book disagrees with me on this point! And I really can't blame them. After all, they are paid to teach you everything they possibly can about their particular subjects. What may surprise you is that every CEO and corporate manager who has proofed this book agrees with me on this point. Why would they agree? The answer lies in the need to *prioritize*, something that they do constantly every day. There is only so much time that you can devote to studying, so you have to prioritize how you are going to spend that time. To use an example, don't burn up your time working show-your-work homework problems when the test will only have fill-in-the-blank and multiple choice questions! That just doesn't make sense. The exception to this is when all of your homework problems are required to be turned in for a grade.

Once you have isolated the homework problems that you intend to work, you're ready for the hard part. Work the problems all the way through without looking in the book or at your notes (unless these sources can be used during the test). If, after repeated attempts you find that you can't work the problems, see #43.

39

WORK THROUGH YOUR OWN PRACTICE TEST
PRIOR TO EVERY ACTUAL TEST

❖   📖   ❖

For me, this was the key step in my study routine and the one that I spent the most time on. After all you have read, I am sure that this doesn't surprise you! Your practice test can come from various sources, as we have discussed earlier. Any source is fine. In many cases, the previous step and this step can be combined. What's important is to have a practice test that is as much like the actual test as possible. Once you have your practice test in front of you, approach taking it just like you would approach taking the actual upcoming test. Don't look at your notes, don't look back in your book and don't do anything that you would not be able to do during the actual test. Once your practice test is completed, check for two things:

40.

ANALYZE THE TIME SPENT
WORKING YOUR PRACTICE TEST

❖ 📖 ❖

Take note of how much time it took to work each problem of your practice test. Now look at your overall time. Did you run longer than the time you will be given? If so, analyze where you need to pick-up the pace. Did you finish with several minutes to spare? If so, analyze where you can slow down and take extra care. Once you make the necessary adjustments, go back and take note of how long it took you to work each type of problem. As you will see in an upcoming tip, knowing this on the front end will help you immensely during the actual test.

41.

GRADE YOUR PRACTICE TEST

❖ 📖 ❖

To achieve the optimum benefit from practicing taking a test, you have to grade yourself as ruthlessly as your instructor will. If your practice test comes from an old test or from homework problems, this won't be difficult at all, as the answers will most likely be provided for you. If you have created your own practice test, go back through your notes, through the text - whatever source you need to look in, and determine if you have worked the problems correctly. Whatever score you receive on your practice test will probably be about the same score you'd receive during the actual test!

Quite often you won't be very happy with your score on your practice test. This is not unusual. It is very common to believe that you are better prepared for a test than you actually are. Practicing taking the test allows you to discover this ahead of time. When you are faced with this situation, there are no easy answers. You have to roll up your sleeves, buckle down and pound through the source of the problem.

42.

START PRACTICING WELL AHEAD OF TIME

❖ 📖 ❖

It will be very tempting to procrastinate and first work through your practice test the night before your actual test. That's too late! You will be taking a major gamble. It is better to practice taking the test at least twice, starting a few days prior to the actual test. At the very latest, work through it two nights before test day, then again the night before. That gives you at least a day to go get the help that you might need. Also, our previous discussion about short- and long-term memory comes into play. By practicing the test more than once, you will commit the method of working those particular type of test problems to long-term memory - always the best option.

43.

GET HELP AS SOON AS YOU NEED IT

❖   📖   ❖

Never, I repeat, *never* be embarrassed to ask for help when you don't understand something. Keeping quiet is ridiculous! Too much money is being spent on your college education for you to fail because you are embarrassed to ask for help. Remember, you are at school to learn, not to walk around confused. When you find yourself in this situation, I suggest that you go directly to the professor. Most professors will post their office hours for the sole purpose of helping students that are having trouble understanding the material. If for some reason you don't feel comfortable speaking with the professor directly, then at least go to a fellow classmate and ask for help.

Remember, confusion is just like a serious illness. If you treat it early on, you have a good chance of curing it. If you let the confusion grow, you will reach a point where there is little or no hope for recovery. Don't let that happen to you.

RE-GROUP EACH WEEK

❖ 📖 ❖

Spend some type of study or review time with every subject at least once a week. If you have a class with homework assignments hitting you left and right and tests being given frequently, this will not be difficult to do. If the class doesn't have a heavy assignment load, you will have to discipline yourself to sit down once a week for a thorough self-review. Remember: finding out that you're lost after three weeks have passed is much more damaging than discovering you're lost after only one week! This is why re-grouping for all subjects on a weekly basis is key.

DON'T BLOW OFF YOUR STUDY ROUTINE
BECAUSE IT SEEMS LIKE TOO MUCH TROUBLE

❖   📖   ❖

The previous steps we covered were my basic study routine when I was in college. I know it seems like a lot, but it really wasn't that much at all. I could run through the above routine for two subjects in the time it took my friends to study for one subject in which they worked needless homework problems and tried to read the entire textbook! It's all about making your routine a habit. It's not going to be fun at first, but give your routine a chance to take root. Once it does, it will seem like no big deal.

Remember, the idea isn't to get out of studying. It's to take the time that you do study and use it effectively. Speaking of using time effectively, that brings us to our next point:

46.

KNOW WHEN TO SAY WHEN

❖ 📖 ❖

This phrase certainly applies to studying. Sometimes you have to face the reality that you are not meant to completely understand every subject you take. I'll use myself as an example. I never, never could do well in physics. No matter how hard I'd study or how many times I went back to the professor, some of the principles of physics just would not click with me - and still don't. If there comes a point when this happens to you, I recommend that you move along to more productive activities. For some, if the problem is serious enough and involves a key subject, it may mean having to take a strong look at your major. You may not be in something that you are naturally suited for, or a field you don't enjoy (see # 8). It's a safe bet that if you don't enjoy your field of study, you won't enjoy making a living at it either! However most of the time, it just means that there are going to be a few subjects that come along that you are not going to do as well in or enjoy as much as others.

When this situation becomes obvious to you, do not let that subject become a black hole into which all of your time is pulled. Give it a fair amount of your attention, then cut your losses and move on to something else. Spend that time on other subjects that need attention or on something else you enjoy more.

All that we have covered in the previous chapters has been leading up to the "main event"; actually **taking the test**. The following suggestions will help you come out a winner every time.

47.

VISUALIZE A POSITIVE OUTCOME

❖ ✍ ❖

I honestly believe that keeping a positive frame of mind and visualizing success can make as much as two letter grades of difference in your test score. Why? Because your state of mind will be your greatest asset or your greatest liability, and the choice is up to you. Remember, if it works on the playing field or in the performance hall, it will work in the classroom. Jack Nicklaus, one of the greatest golfers of our time, practices the same visualization exercise before every shot he plays. Prior to making a shot, he visualizes himself making the best possible shot. He imagines that his stance, his swing, his stroke and his follow-through are all executed perfectly. He then visualizes the ball's travel path, with the perfect trajectory, landing in just the right place. And he does this before every shot! Jack Nicklaus has learned from experience the immense power of the mind to affect a positive outcome. You can apply this same technique to taking a test, and, trust me, it works. Visualize entering the classroom with confidence, taking your seat and answering each question in just the right amount of time, giving the perfect answer in every case. Carry that confident feeling with you into the classroom at test time and play to win it all. You will be amazed at the difference this one technique will make.

48.

GET A GOOD NIGHT'S SLEEP

As we discussed in #17, all-nighters are a lousy way to prepare for a test. Don't place yourself in the situation where you feel you need to pull an all-nighter, or even stay up past your normal bedtime. In order to perform at an optimum level, you need to be completely rested, not stressed out and tense from a lack of sleep. Lying in bed before falling asleep is the perfect time to practice the positive visualization technique described in the previous point. Instead of allowing the pre-test stress to keep you tossing and turning all night, your positive outlook will help you get the rest you will need.

49.

LOOK OVER THE TEST BEFORE PLUNGING IN

❖ ✍ ❖

You should do this every single time you take a test. If you don't, you could very well get caught running out of time. Remember, if you practice taking the test ahead of time, you will know how long it will take to work each type of problem. Give yourself a time limit to spend on each problem. If you start to run out of time on a particular problem and the answer is not coming to you, don't freeze - just move on to the next problem. When you have worked all the problems you can, go back to the problem you skipped and try again.

50

TELL THEM EVERYTHING THAT YOU KNOW

This is essential for tests with discussion questions and show-your-work problems. For the latter, be sure to state your assumption before working the problem, even if you're not convinced it's the right assumption! Work the problem based on your assumption, carefully presenting your answer to match the professor's expectations of structure. And no matter what, BE NEAT! You'd be surprised how many points are lost on tests just because of sloppy penmanship. Don't self-edit unless you're sure you're giving enough information. By self-edit, I mean the practice of not putting something down because you think it's not necessary. If you're not sure you've provided the whole answer, then put down any and every thing that you feel may in some way contribute towards the ultimate answer of the question.

51

TRY TO ANSWER EVERY QUESTION TO SOME EXTENT
(THE NAME OF THE GAME IS TO SCORE POINTS)

❖ ✍ ❖

Again, this is essential for discussion questions and show-your-work problems. Remember that an unanswered question is automatically not correct. A partially answered question at least has a chance of being partially correct. Therefore, even if you are absolutely convinced that you do not know the answer to a question, try to answer it anyway. Maybe you aren't giving yourself enough credit (pardon the pun). It won't seem so stupid if you are given a few points of partial credit which wind up making a letter grade of difference on the test! Going back to a previous point, this is where the true beauty of practicing taking a show-your-work test comes in. If you take the time to structure an answer to a test problem in the manner that a professor is accustomed to, you will often get partial credit even if the answer is not correct! Practicing taking the test allows you to work on answering questions using proper structure. There were many times that I missed the same number of questions as did some of my classmates based on content, but because I used proper structure, I often scored a letter grade higher.

As the subtitle suggests, the name of the game is to score points. Start at zero and focus on the points you're accruing, rather than subtracting points from 100. By using this approach, you will work from a positive mind set instead of a negative one.

52.

LEAVE ENOUGH TIME TO
CAREFULLY REVIEW YOUR WORK

❖ ✍ ❖

I shake my head when I think of how many times I turned in a test early, convinced that I aced it, only to get it back with a low grade because of careless mistakes. Has that ever happened to you? Don't let it happen again. Take all the time you are allotted and look over your work carefully. Refer back to #40 about timing yourself during the practice test. The idea is to have enough time left over to carefully go back over each problem and check for errors - not to leave the class early.

53.

WHEN IT'S OVER, IT'S OVER

❖ 🖎 ❖

This means just what it says. Some of my college friends would let the experience of taking a challenging test ruin the rest of their day, worrying themselves sick about how they did. Don't dwell on a test after you have taken it. You'll find out how you did soon enough. Enjoy the rest of your day.

54

CORRECT YOUR MISTAKES
WHEN YOU GET THE TEST BACK

❖ ✍ ❖

This essential step is overlooked by many. A test with a bunch of wrong answers on it is not much good to anyone! On the other hand, a test with all answers correct makes a great study aid for finals as well as a helpful information source to lend to others in the future (see #29).

PREPARING FOR A COMPREHENSIVE FINAL EXAM -
USE WHAT YOU ALREADY HAVE

❖ ✍ ❖

Final exam week is the toughest week of the term you'll face. Finals often account for a large portion of your grade in a class. Stress levels are at an all-time high, and your ability to take tests is put to the ultimate test. If you have been following a good study routine, such as the one discussed earlier, you're in great shape. Most of the information you'll need for your finals is already stored away in long-term memory. All you will need to do is stimulate it a little!

Use all of your corrected tests (see previous point) to prepare a practice final exam. Before taking it, skim over your notes and analyze your previous tests in great detail. Work through your practice final and repeat this procedure until you are happy with your performance. When you reach this point, sit back, smile, and be thankful you aren't staying up all night like many of your friends!

PLAN FOR AND GET
THE CLASSES YOU WANT

On most college campuses, class registration is one of the most frustrating processes you will ever go through. You have your heart set on that Tuesday, Thursday class at 9:30 with that great professor and what do you get - a Monday, Wednesday, Friday class at 2:00 with the worst professor in the department! Sound familiar? Well, fear not! Here are three ways to make registration a positive process:

56.

PLAN AHEAD

❖ ☑ ❖

Before registration day, obtain a class schedule, and map out exactly which classes you want. For each class, come up with a second choice - what you will settle for if you can't get your first choice. Study how opting for a second choice affects the rest of your schedule. Make sure that you can come up with at least three or four acceptable combinations. This way, you can react quickly during the scheduling process, instead of panicking and making a rash decision you will regret later.

57.

GO TO THE PROFESSOR IF NECESSARY

❖ ☑ ❖

If the class you had your heart set on is full, and no alternative seems reasonable, go straight to the professor whose class you are interested in. When I was in college, before the days of computer-based class scheduling, I tried this approach. After being told that a class I wanted was closed, I went to the professor's office and talked with him. I explained that I thought he was the best teacher for me and that I would appreciate anything he could do to get me into his class. Steps were taken to have me added to the class, even though it was listed as closed. These days, this approach may sound impossible, but I recommend you give it a try for two reasons. First, you never know what is possible until you try. Second, at the very least, chances are that the professor will be flattered enough to invite you to come to him anytime you need assistance outside the classroom. In essence, you will get your own preferred tutor!

58.

CLOSELY MONITOR THE DROP/ADD SYSTEM

❖ ☑ ❖

Check daily with the department scheduler until the last day one is eligible to drop and add a class. Many times you will find that the particular class (and professor) you want has had someone drop the class. Don't delay! If your schedule permits, add the class you want immediately, then drop the one you're in. Again, don't kid yourself. If the professor is the best one for you, it will be worth the effort and will pay off in the long run. If changing classes creates a scheduling conflict, you will have to weigh the benefit of adding one class over dropping another. If your drop/add system requires that you put your name on a waiting list, then the key for you is to put your name on that list the moment you find out that the class is full. This is another case where timing is everything.

BUYING BOOKS

When I was in college, I wound up spending more on textbooks than I should have; particularly during my freshman year. You don't have to let that happen to you. Before you purchase a textbook please take the following steps:

59.

FIND OUT HOW THE PROFESSOR
PLANS TO USE THE TEXT

Find out from each professor how he or she plans to utilize the text. Will it be a key source of information for the class or will the book stay unopened the whole semester? Perhaps the professor will prefer to have you study notes taken during lectures instead. If this is the case, why buy one? Remember, if you begin to feel awkward because you don't have a text, you can always borrow or buy one later. (An exception would be textbooks you wish to have for future reference purposes in your career. In those few cases, these books are worth the investment.)

60.

BUY USED TEXTBOOKS IF POSSIBLE

I realize that sometimes this is not possible because the professor requires a text that is a new edition, but many times used books are feasible. Look for used books at your college bookstore. Look at ads in your school newspaper. See if your university has a student book exchange. These are all viable ways that you can locate a used text for a fraction of the cost of a new text. Also, never forget that borrowing a text is free!

61.

SELL TEXTBOOKS YOU DON'T WANT TO KEEP

❖ ‿ ❖

In my case, this was almost all of them! The best time is before the next term begins. This is the optimum time to make a sale, hopefully before professors change editions. Your objective should be to recoup as much of your textbook investment as possible, so that when your college days are over, you will have only spent hundreds, rather than thousands of dollars on textbooks.

FOUR MORE COLLEGE-BASED TIPS

62

PARTICIPATE IN COOPERATIVE EDUCATION

If I could name just one change I'd like to see at the college level, it would be for all students to participate in some form of cooperative education. Cooperative education, also known as co-oping or interning, allows you to get practical work experience related to your field of study at a sponsoring company. Work terms occur at regularly spaced intervals, usually every other semester or quarter, although some internships are strictly summer assignments.

The immediate benefits of a co-op program are enormous. First, you will perform better in your related classes, since you will have seen first hand what's being taught in the classroom. Second, you can pay for a large part of your tuition and other expenses from your work earnings. Third and most important, you will have developed a real-world wisdom and good, relevant work experience prior to graduation.

The long-term benefits are even better. Co-op experience gives you an incredible edge in the job market. You are practically a shoe-in for permanent employment with your co-op company, and in general, most companies favor candidates with practical, on-the-job experience. I can't help but be biased - I was a co-op student and I know my work experience played a major role in the career opportunities I had. If there are any drawbacks, they would be that you are away from school and the social atmosphere every other term, and that it usually takes an extra year to graduate. Believe me, it's worth it.

After all, what's your hurry? Please check into cooperative education at your school. Get all the information you can, and make the decision that's best for you. If cooperative education or some type of internship program is not available for your major, find out why not. Cooperative education is definitely worth your strong consideration.

63.

PARTICIPATE IN EXTRACURRICULAR ACTIVITIES

A common way "the system" can control you is when you find yourself becoming reluctant to participate in outside activities you enjoy because you feel compelled to study all the time. This is a BIG mistake! You can't hope to achieve balance in your life if all you focus on are academics. The study methods described previously are designed to help you to free up time for other things. Take advantage of it.

Remember, college life is like anything else; you get out of it what you put into it. Get involved! Care about where you go to school. Join and participate in student organizations that you feel really make a difference on your campus. Leave your mark and make a significant contribution through your efforts. It's something you'll be proud of, and, as a side benefit, you will build a strong record of extracurricular achievement that will really pay off when you are trying to land a job.

64.

TAKE A LEADERSHIP ROLE

Just as your GPA is an indication of your dedication to success and willingness to work hard, involvement in extracurricular activities serves as an equally important indicator. This type of involvement indicates strong interpersonal skills, an outgoing nature, and leadership potential, particularly if you've held an office such as president, vice-president, etc., of an organization. Most top-level careers require employees with proven leadership and team-building skills. Extracurricular activities are your chance to shine and develop these skills. As an upperclassman, make plans to assume such an leadership role and dedicate your group to a task that will make a real difference. Everyone involved and everyone affected will benefit.

A word of caution, however: I am not advocating "padding your resume" with lots of extracurricular activities in which you never lift a finger to do anything except belong to them. Recruiters will see right through this. Most recruiters will have made a point to find out ahead of time which organizations on your campus involve effort and which ones do not. Padded resumes are not impressive. Resumes which reflect real effort are.

65

GREEKS, ETC. -- MAKE RESPONSIBLE CHOICES

Most colleges and universities have fraternities and sororities or organizations similar to them. These organizations can be a very positive part of your college life. "Greek" (fraternity/sorority) life provides you a forum to make close friendships with people you can relate to and helps you build strong interpersonal skills necessary to succeed after college.

However, for some people, fraternity and sorority life can cause more harm than good. This is usually the case when a student lets Greek life overshadow the main reason for going to college in the first place.

Fond memories of four years of partying will fade quickly if, after graduation, you find yourself without a job, or with a job you had to settle for because you weren't properly prepared.

Greek life is not for everyone. Don't feel pressured to belong to a Greek organization just because "everybody else is doing it." Choose organizations and activities that you want to participate in. There are certainly dozens of other excellent organizations that have nothing to do with the Greek system. Don't let anyone dictate to you what you should or should not do with your social life.

If you choose the Greek life, enjoy it to its fullest and make a point to help run the show. Be sure to always keep in proper perspective where Greek life fits in with the rest of your college life. It's all about control.

Make sure you're always in control; don't let any organization control you.

TIME MANAGEMENT

❖ 🕐 ❖

The laws of nature unfortunately don't budge when it comes to the concept of time - at least not for us day to day! Every week has seven days, every day has 24 hours, and to make matters worse, we're designed to have to shut down for maintenance five to eight hours every 24 hour cycle. That would be no big deal if those professors you pay to teach you stuff and those organizations and jobs you're involved in would go easy on you. Forget that! So what can you do? Learn to efficiently manage the time you have. The following three tips should help:

66.

MAKE "TO DO" LISTS –
ONE FOR THE WEEK AND ONE FOR EACH DAY

❖ 🕐 ❖

This is just a master list of all the things you have to do that day. By taking the time to sit down and write out these lists, you will organize your thoughts, begin prioritizing the tasks, and have a master guide to go by so you won't forget anything. Check off your items as you complete them; it gives you a great feeling of accomplishment and helps your mind move on to the next task. I couldn't get through a typical day without a "To Do" list. Trust me, they work!

67.

GET A DAY PLANNER AND USE IT

❖ 🕐 ❖

A day planner is a small booklet that contains a calendar with room to write out your main appointments and tasks either on the calendar itself or down the side of the calendar page. There are different brands, and all basically have the same stuff. You can get sheets that cover a day at a glance, week at a glance, month at a glance or all three. The point is to use your planner in conjunction with your "To Do" lists to help you stay organized and prioritized. You'll be surprised how much time you actually do have in your day when you schedule your activities in a planner. Carry it with you throughout the day and refer to it often.

68.

PLAN YOUR DAY
IN A QUIET PLACE AT A QUIET TIME

❖ 🕐 ❖

I am accustomed to planning the coming day in the morning. My wife likes to plan her day the night before. Perhaps you'll like to plan your day in the evening before or after dinner. What is important is to plan your day when you are relaxed and can think clearly. It is also helpful to plan your day the same time every day. This will turn your planning into a habit. Use your day planner and write out your "To Do" lists at this time, prioritizing as you go. Before long, you will be effortlessly accomplishing twice as much each day as your friends do, and they'll be lining up to seek your advice!

MANAGING MONEY

❖ $ ❖

69.

PREPARE A MONTHLY BUDGET

❖ **$** ❖

It is important for you to begin budgeting your expenses while in college. Not only is it a habit that you should follow for the rest of your life, it will help you immensely right here and now. It's not hard to do, it just takes the self-discipline to start. Begin by writing down all of your monthly fixed expenses. Fixed expenses are those that don't change - student loan payment, rent, car payment, etc. Then, analyze your last several months of "usual and customary" expenses. These include utilities, phone, food, gas, and so forth. Determine your average usual and customary expense amount for each category, and add it to your fixed expenses list. Total everything up. This is what I call your starting point monthly budget. Is the total acceptable? It usually isn't! The next step is to determine where you can cut back on your spending. (For our family, the two categories we knew we had to cut back on were food and phone usage.) Try to get your monthly total down as low as possible, within reason. Be careful not to cut your monthly total so low that you've doomed yourself to fail. Once you have number you are comfortable with, you have a monthly budget!

70.

TRACK YOUR MONTHLY EXPENSES

❖ $ ❖

Enter your new budget on a spreadsheet, with the categories down the side. In the next column, write in your budget numbers for each category. Now all you have to do is keep track of your spending. At the end of each week, or twice a month, write down what you've spent by category. Total across at the end of the month and see how your actual spending compares to your budgeted amounts. Where did you go over? Where did you save? In cases where you exceeded your goals, determine what adjustments to make in the coming month to bring that category of spending in line. In cases where you saved, keep an eye out in the coming months for repeated savings in this category. If you consistently come in under budget, lower your budget accordingly.

71.

TRY THE ENVELOPE METHOD
OF EXPENSE MANAGEMENT

❖ **$** ❖

If you find that you're not able to hold your spending
in line with your budget, and you've determined that
your budget goals are indeed reasonable, you may
want to give the envelope method a try. First, set up a
file with an envelope for each budget category; e.g. an
envelope marked "Food", etc. At the beginning of
each month, put play money (or the real thing if you
can keep the file locked) into each envelope in the
amount equal to each budgeted amount. If you've set
aside $40 a month for gas, put $40 in the "Gas"
envelope, and so on. As a spending need arises during

the month, take the money out of the appropriate envelope, either symbolically or actual currency.

(If you're using play money, put the money you take out into another envelope marked "Spent" so you can recycle it for next time.) At this point, sticking to your budget is basically a no-brainer. When an envelope is empty, simply don't spend any more against that category for the rest of the month, no matter how uncomfortable that may be. No matter what, DON'T BORROW MONEY FROM A FIXED EXPENSE ENVELOPE TO USE FOR ANOTHER PURPOSE. The envelope method has worked wonders for people when nothing else would. If you think it will help you, try it and let me know how you make out.

72.

PAY YOUR BILLS ON TIME, NO MATTER WHAT

❖ $ ❖

The temptation will arise to put off paying a bill now and then so you can spend the money on something else more tempting. Don't give in! Other than a legitimate emergency, there is nothing more pressing than paying what you owe on time. You may wonder why it really matters; after all these are big companies with deep pockets - they can wait, right? That's not the point. The point is something called your credit rating. There are national information systems called credit bureaus that keep track of how faithfully you pay what you owe. When you fail to pay a bill promptly or not at all, this is recorded by a credit bureau. A poor credit rating can dog you for the rest of your life and is very difficult to get cleared. Trying to get any kind of loan in the future - a car, business or home loan - will be difficult if not impossible if you have a poor credit rating. And to think it started with some late or unpaid bills in college! Believe me, it's not worth it. Pay your bills on time.

73.

AVOID THE CREDIT CARD TRAP

❖ $ ❖

Between your ongoing need for funds and bank card companies throwing cards at you left and right, it's easy to get sucked into the credit card trap. We're talking financial quicksand here; you can get in over your head before you know it. Unfortunately, the answer to the credit card dilemma isn't simple. If used responsibly, credit cards can serve a useful purpose. A credit card provides a means of identification, and its proper use by a first-time holder will result in the creation of a valuable asset - a good credit rating. However, if used irresponsibly, a credit card will cause damage that, as we discussed previously, will haunt you for many years to come. Whether or not a student should obtain a credit card depends entirely on the maturity and financial responsibility of the individual.

I asked Bob Reid, CEO of First Union National Bank of Pennsylvania, to give us his advice on this issue. Here are his suggestions:

1. If you are a freshman, or if you depend upon your parents or guardians for financial assistance, first obtain their permission prior to applying for a card.

2. Your credit card purchases should involve usual and customary expenses that you can pay off in full at the end of each month. Translation: If you do not think that you will be able to always pay

off your card in full each month, don't get a credit card.

3. In the event of an unforeseen emergency expense, use your credit card ONLY if you can have the debt paid off completely within three months.

4. One credit card is enough. Shop around to obtain the lowest interest rate possible.

Keep in mind that the interest rates attached to credit cards are the highest on the market. If it appears that your expenses will exceed your income on an ongoing basis, and borrowing money is your only answer, DO NOT turn to a credit card. A conventional student loan is a much safer and smarter way to borrow.

74.

START SAVING NOW

❖ **$** ❖

What?! You must be thinking, "Is this guy nuts?!"
Well, before you disown all of my advice, let me
explain. There's a wonderful concept you will learn if
you take an economics course called "The principle of
compounding over time". What this means is that the
longer you save money without touching it, the more
it will grow. The longer you wait, the more rapidly
your savings grow.   If left alone until you're
retirement age, the amount you will accumulate from
a regular little saving plan will absolutely astound you.
Well, to benefit from this wonderful compounding
principle, you have to start saving as early as possible,

and contributing toward your savings should happen every month like clockwork. College is the time to start, even if you owe money against student loans, for two reasons. First, the few years' jump you get by not waiting until after college makes a very real difference in the amount you eventually accumulate. Second, you will begin the saving habit now. If you wait, you may fail to get into the habit for years. The amount doesn't have to be much - even $20 a month is fine. The point is to get into the habit.

Note: What this book does not cover are the many different types of savings options you have. Check with your parents, banker, or someone else whose financial advice you trust prior to making this decision. Make it soon, though, and start saving!

75

PAY YOURSELF FIRST

❖ **$** ❖

The way to make sure you consistently put money into your savings is to always pay yourself first, before you pay any other monthly bills. Treat your savings contribution just like a fixed expense bill, one that can absolutely not be put off. Once you become more financially stable, or if you have a steady job right now, you may want to consider having this amount taken out of your checking account by automatic draft. This will guarantee that you never miss a month, but you will need to remember to record the withdrawal in your check book each month. Either way, you will find that saving will become an automatic process that requires little thought. Years from now, you'll thank me from the bottom of your bank account!

LIFE-STYLE STUFF

76.

WORK ON YOUR WEAK POINTS

Let's face it. There are just some things we're better at than others, some things we enjoy more than others. There's nothing wrong with that, unless what a person's not so good at is a skill needed for future success. For example, whenever I speak to college students, I ask for a show of hands as to who in the audience, if given the chance, would like to trade places with me; in other words, who enjoys public speaking. Usually, about a third of the hands in the audience go up. I then ask the opposite question, who would rather be doing just about anything other than trading places with me. Another third of the hands go up. Then I ask the whole audience the clincher: how many have taken or intend to take a public speaking class? Take a wild guess whose hands don't go up. That's right, the students who don't enjoy public speaking! Now, what's wrong with this picture?

College is the perfect place to do the hard thing and work on your weak points. To use our example, public speaking may never be something you love, but you will be helped immensely by working on this skill now, rather than later on the job. The same idea holds true for any number of things. As you read this, you're probably already thinking about what areas of yours could use some work. Are there opportunities at your school to address these weaknesses? If so, take a deep breath and dive in!

77.

IF YOU DRINK, DRINK RESPONSIBLY

I promised myself when I wrote this book that I would try not to sound "preachy", but bear with me on this point and the next one. If you don't drink, good for you; you can skip this one. If you do, or think that you want to, read on. First off, if you're not of legal drinking age, don't drink. The trouble you could wind up in could cost you your entire future, and it's not worth it. There is a time and a place. You know it and I know it. It seems like lots of folks think that since they're at college, "time and place" should be translated into "anytime, any place"! You're not stupid. You know that drinking to excess is a bone head move for a whole host of reasons. Drinking to excess while you're trying to prepare yourself for the rest of your life is insane! If you are of legal drinking age, and you do consume alcoholic beverages, here's some good, road-tested advice to follow that I promise you'll thank me for later:

Don't drink during the week or any day/evening you have class the next day.

On weekends or weeknights that you don't have class the next day, if you're going to drink, do so in moderation.

Getting blasted doesn't bring out your best qualities in front of people you have to face the next day, not to mention the lovely feeling it gives you later. Don't do it.

Don't ever, and I mean EVER, drink alone. If you have been or think that you need to, chances are that you have a drinking dependency. Go get help immediately. (A drinking dependency is nothing to be ashamed of, and untreated, will ruin your life present and future. Please don't put off checking it out.)

Never, EVER drink before or while driving.

Enough said.

78.

AVOID DRUGS

It seems ridiculous that I would even have to put this piece of advice in this book. In fact, the only reason I did was to clearly state my position on the subject and encourage you to help any friends who may be involved with drugs. I mean, let's face it - if you care enough to read this book in the first place, then you are well aware that only a complete fool would put their entire future at risk by experimenting with or using any type of illegal drug (or abusing legal ones). If you happen to know someone who is, help the person take a step back and look at the long-term impact of his or her behavior. Ask the person to stop, and if necessary, to seek help. Then, take the important and often overlooked next step. Follow-up with the person regularly until you see a real change.

79

SERIOUS RELATIONSHIPS - KEEP YOUR BALANCE

There's no doubt about it; whoever wrote the old song "Love is in the air" must have been talking about colleges! For many of you, college will be a time of romance and getting bit by the "serious" love bug. There's certainly nothing wrong with that; many a successful marriage has come of such relationships. However, if you're not careful, you'll take your eye off the ball regarding your studies and other activities, and that could spell trouble for your future. Either or both of you can slip into the "nothing in the world matters but you" trap. Setting some ground rules can help you avoid this situation, and keep your relationship healthy, too. As I said earlier about drinking, there is a time and a place. Now that I think about it, my advice about drinking translates well here, with a few modifications. On nights with classes the next day, if you have to see each other in order keep the world from spinning out of control, etc., do it in a productive way. In other words, study together! Try to restrict the most time-consuming social activities with each other to the weekends or nights before a light class day. Remember - true love waits. If you have to spend some time apart so that one or the other of you can get an important project done or study for an upcoming test, you'll live. Don't allow forced togetherness stand in the way of all else. Trust me, nothing good will come of that on any front.

80.

PEER PRESSURE - KEEP IT IN PERSPECTIVE

A college student wrote to me with the following dilemma:

"When arriving at a new school, it is very difficult to adjust to the new environment. How can one prioritize in the face of peer pressure - in other words, how can you decide when to tell your friends to party without you when you want to get along with them and still maintain good grades?"

Can you relate? I think most of us can. Here's how I answered her question:

"That's a tough situation to find yourself in, particularly when you are new to the college life. True, peer pressure is a big factor for you now, but it will become less important over time. Think about your dilemma this way: if the end of the year rolls around and you have a low GPA to show for it, how will you feel? I doubt you'll be thinking, '"Oh well, it was worth it to party more with my friends"! The key concept to grasp here is that success in college is a choice, and it's yours to make. Keep in mind that your GPA this semester or quarter will average into your overall GPA from now on. Am I saying you shouldn't party? Of course not. With careful planning, you can work out a schedule where you can set aside time to blow off the books and also maintain a consistent, effective study schedule. Prediction: Before long, your friends will begin to admire your self-discipline and ask for pointers on how to be as organized as you are."

81.

TAKE FREQUENT WALKS
OUTSIDE OF THE IVORY TOWER

Back in my corporate recruiting days, one of the colleges at which we recruited was a large urban university in our city. After a favorable interview on campus, it is customary to hold a second interview on the company premises. Consistently, and to my amazement, our recruits from this school had no idea how to find our offices in the downtown area, just three miles away! Why? Because the only world they knew existed within the walls of their college. The term "ivory tower" is used to describe this isolation of students and faculty from the "real" world, and it's not usually a term used in a positive light. I urge you to get to know and become involved in the community that exists beyond your campus. If you will, everybody wins! You'll have a more accurate and balanced perspective, you'll be enriched from the experience of being a part of a larger and more diverse community, and your community will be enriched because of your contributions.

82.

PRACTICE RANDOM ACTS OF KINDNESS

College marks your entry into the world of independent living. As we've said before, you are now in control of your life. One of the best habits you can develop now is to practice random acts of kindness. Perhaps you've seen bumper stickers with this message, or heard this phrase in passing. There is plenty of pain and suffering to go around in life. You have the power to make the lives of those around you a little bit better every single day. It doesn't require a lot effort; just keep your eyes open and offer some assistance when you can. To give you an example, some folks routinely make a point to reactivate parking meters that have expired so the owners of the cars in question won't get a ticket. A friend of mine helps out serving food at the homeless mission in town a couple times a month. Little things like opening the door for another, picking up litter you see on your way to class, helping a student pick up dropped books or simply offering a smile of encouragement to someone who appears to be having a bad day - all have a deeper impact than what you see on the surface. Two wonderful things happen every time you practice a random act of kindness. First, you feel rewarded on a level that can't be matched. Second, and most important, your act of kindness will inspire those whose lives you touch to do the same. The possibilities are endless. Do your part and enjoy!

83.

AVOID BURN-OUT

Particularly in American culture, we tend to go and go and go until we finally burn ourselves to a crisp. When we do this, we rob ourselves physically, mentally, emotionally and spiritually. Think of yourself as if you were a machine. There are two ways to use machines. You can run continuously until the machine finally breaks down, which not only causes permanent damage, but makes using the machine up until the break-down point harder and harder. The alternative is to take the machine down for preventive maintenance on a scheduled, routine basis, then continue on at top speed and efficiency. College is the perfect place to learn how to take time out for yourself on regular intervals to rest, relax and rejuvenate. Think long-term and you'll see how much sense it makes to avoid burn-out!

THE JOB INTERVIEW

84

WHAT EMPLOYERS ARE LOOKING FOR

As a former corporate recruiter, I am frequently asked what employers are looking for. As we discussed previously, an employer's first impression of you will be in the form of an application or resume. The three main categories evaluated are academic performance, work experience and extracurricular involvement. Based on the combined strength of these three components, interview selections are made. During the interview, the skills you have developed related to the three preceding points are explored and evaluated in more depth. Additional criteria are also evaluated, including your ability to communicate, ability to think quickly on your feet, overall strength of your interpersonal skills and last, but not least, determining if you will be a good "fit" at the company. I realize that the last point in particular is a very subjective measure, but nevertheless is a factor in determining which candidates ultimately receive offers.

85.

THE JOB INTERVIEW -- IT'S A BIG DEAL

Your last major activity prior to leaving college is the process of interviewing for a job. The great majority of college careers span four or five years. It has always amazed me how those four or five years ultimately boil down to twenty or thirty minutes in a job interview. Without question, it's some of the most important time you will ever spend up to that point in your lifetime. I know that sounds pretty heavy, and it should. Job interviews are not to be taken lightly. The path you start out on for the rest of your life all begins with a job interview. Hundreds of books have been written on how to prepare a resume and interview for a job (what to do, what not to do, what to say, what not to say, how to look, how not to look, etc.). What I have to tell you is brief, but like this book's title, goes straight to the point.

86

THE THREE ELEMENTS OF THE JOB INTERVIEW

A job interview basically consists of three elements: the interviewer, the interviewee (that's you) and your record. That's it. Everything we have talked about previously focused on actions you can take that will eventually be reflected on your record. Therefore, when your senior year rolls around and it's time to interview for jobs, your record is basically set in stone. There is not much you can do to change it. You can change the format of your resume a little, rearrange this and that, but the substance can't change. The interviewer is another part of the interview that you have no control over. You won't know anything about his background, what he likes and doesn't like, what he believes in and doesn't believe in, or if he's in a good mood or bad mood! All of this is beyond your control. That means there is only one component you can control - you and how you present yourself during the job interview.

87.

PREPARE AHEAD OF TIME WITH BASIC RESEARCH

Be sure to visit your placement office a few days before your interview and review any information about the company that's available. Some companies have representatives conduct information sessions or speak at club meetings on campus prior to interview day. You should take advantage of these events if at all possible. You should have a good basic understanding of what the company does, where it does what it does, its product line, and its philosophy. From this information, you'll be able to prepare some good questions to ask during the interview.

Don't do exhaustive research - quoting from the annual report isn't necessary!

88.

TAKE PRIDE IN YOUR APPEARANCE, YET LOOK COMFORTABLE

You want to look as nice as you can when you participate in a job interview. Dress in business attire (not casual clothes). Get a good night's sleep so you won't look tired and find yourself having the incredible urge to yawn while the interviewer is talking to you! (Apply those visualization techniques we discussed in #47 the night before.)

On the other hand, the most expensive suit of clothes in the world and the most fashionable hair style won't do a thing for you if you look uptight and uncomfortable. Get used to the clothes that you will be interviewing in before the interview. Don't let interview day be the first day you have ever worn a particular outfit. You want the interviewer to notice your appearance but not dwell on it. If you are uncomfortable, the interviewer will notice and he will try to figure out why you're uncomfortable. All the while the interviewer won't be spending time on the more important objective - your qualifications for the position.

89.

MAKE EYE CONTACT FREQUENTLY

You must approach every interview with confidence. Don't be afraid to look the interviewer in the eye. It's hard for an interviewer to be impressed with a candidate when the interviewer can't establish eye contact during the course of the interview! Lack of eye contact implies a lack of basic self-confidence. No one wants to hire someone with a lack of self-confidence. It's that simple. If you are uncomfortable with eye contact, confide in a friend and ask the friend to role play with you until you can make eye contact comfortably.

90.

IF YOU'RE NOTICEABLY NERVOUS, ADMIT IT

❖ ❖

It's okay to be nervous. Nervousness is an understandable initial reaction in an interview. If you are feeling extremely nervous at the beginning of an interview, again, be honest and tell the interviewer how you're feeling, then put it behind you and get on with the business at hand.

91.

BE YOURSELF

I know you have heard this one a million times but it honestly is true. The only way you will be able to relax and feel comfortable is if you are being yourself and not trying to put on an act. An interviewer can see through an act immediately and your chances of getting the job will drop significantly. And they should. Think about it. If you have to put on an act in order to get a job then you are probably not interviewing for the right type of position for you in the first place. You want someone to hire you, not someone you are pretending to be.

92.

ANSWER EVERY QUESTION HONESTLY

The great bulk of an interview will be you answering questions of the interviewer. Questions will focus on your personal background, interests, educational background, extracurricular activities and work experiences. In every case, tell the truth. Lying to make yourself look better will not work. Your body language will give you away every time. It's just not worth the risk. If an interviewer even gets the hint that an applicant is not being truthful, she will automatically reject that applicant. The interview may continue on, but in truth, it's already over! It is much better to answer every question honestly and sincerely.   Your truthfulness will show, and remember, honesty is a quality that every company looks for in an employee.

93.

GIVE EXAMPLES

Many interviewers will ask you situational questions. The interviewer will paint a certain scenario and ask you how you would act in such a scenario. In every case, don't hesitate to give examples of actual situations you have been involved in that will help drive home your answer. For example, the interviewer may ask, "Tell me how you would handle a situation in which a seemingly impossible goal has been set for your work team and failure is not an option." You should be prepared to discuss a related situation from your work experience or involvement in an organization that clearly illustrates that you understand the question, have in fact encountered a similar situation, and learned from the experience. Whether or not you were a hero in your example doesn't matter. What matters is that you have experience in real-world situations, learned from your experience and are able to share what you've learned with the interviewer. As you can see, having relevant work experience and a strong record of organizational leadership helps greatly during the interview process. Without these experiences, you will have to answer situational questions "cold", which is much more difficult.

94.

BE SELFISH

❖ 👎👍 ❖

This is my last piece of advice for you regarding job interviews, and though it may sound a bit overboard, I mean it. There is no time when it's more important to be selfish than when you are in a job interview. Interviewers are notorious for asking "Why do you think we should hire you to work for our company?" or "What do you have to offer our company?" In fact, I have often asked the same questions. These questions are valid and you should be prepared to answer them. However, you should be evaluating the company at the same time, seeking the answers to very similar questions. "Why should I work for this company?" "What does this company have to offer me?" You may or may not feel comfortable verbalizing these questions during the actual interview; a lot depends on how the interview is progressing and the personality of the interviewer. Either way, you should be constantly evaluating the company throughout the entire process. Even if you are not a selfish person by nature, the interviewing process is definitely when you need to force yourself to take a selfish stance. Your entire future will be shaped by the employment decision you make. You will have spent an entire college career working to impress a potential employer. Once you've had the opportunity to "show your stuff" during the interview, it's time for the potential employer to impress you.

SOME FINAL THOUGHTS

95.

YOU ARE NOT ALONE

Look around you on your way to your next class. See all of those people? They're in the same boat you are! Don't let yourself become isolated in that sea of bodies walking around you. Those bodies have faces and behind those faces are real people with the same hopes, fears and dreams that you have. Make the effort to reach out and get to know your fellow students. When you face a challenge together with others, you get the feeling that you can accomplish anything. When it's you against the world, every challenge seems overwhelming. Think about it, decide how you'd rather feel, then reach out!

96

MAKE TIME FOR THE LITTLE THINGS

We live in a fast-paced culture; in fact, there's no culture in the world that moves faster. As your graduation nears, you're going to be restless. (It must be the way racehorses must feel in the gate waiting for the bell to ring!) Once your college days are over, you want to Go! Go! Go! If you don't make a special effort, you will get caught up in the rat race immediately. Try to force yourself to make time to appreciate the "little things" you encounter along the way. Take a walk in the woods. Watch a sunset with your significant other. Plant a garden. Read a story to a child. Go to church. These are just a few examples.

Make up your own list of "little things" not to miss out on as you race through your working life. You might just discover that the "little things" aren't so little after all.

97.

CHOICES - A STUDY IN SHADES OF GRAY

Life is about choices. We make hundreds of them every day. With every passing year, I become more and more convinced that choices are not ever black and white; but rather varying shades of gray. What does this mean? Well, it means that when you make a choice, particularly an important one, there's going to be baggage attached. Picture a two-sided scale with the reasons to choose one way on the right side and the reasons to choose the other way on the left. We have to accept that there will always be two sides to every choice. So, how do we choose? By watching which way the scale tips, and picking the side that outweighs the other. A lot of the time, the scale is only going to tip slightly. Those are the hardest choices to make, but we have to make them anyway. My advice: once you make a choice, don't second-guess yourself. As long as you've carefully evaluated your options, take comfort in knowing that you made the best possible decision given the information you had available at the time. Warning! Life has a mean way of making other information available to us after we make a choice that, had we had that information before, we might have made a different choice. If you dwell on this every time it happens, you'll be filled with regret 24 hours a day! Don't fall into that trap. Keep your eyes focused straight ahead and move on.

98.

LIFE IS A CONTACT SPORT

This is a familiar phrase in the business world, and one that you need to understand now. The overall message here is that life is a "who you know" ball game. You will find, particularly after you begin your journey in the world of work, that many of your future opportunities will come about directly as a result of the relationships you build along the way. Like it or not, you can't go it alone in this world. We are designed to spend our lives interacting with others. The process of making the effort to meet people, and through these contacts, helping others meet a need or seeking to have your own needs met is called networking. If you are by nature an extroverted individual, this process will come quite naturally to you. If you are more of an introvert, you have a couple of options. The first is to make a real effort to get out there and meet people anyway, no matter how uncomfortable it initially makes you. You may learn that meeting new people isn't as bad as you think. Your other option is to turn to one of your extroverted friends and ask for help! Either way, you will find that networking with others will be a key to your future success.

99.

PURSUE LIFE-LONG LEARNING

When you have as much stuff piled on top of you as you do right now, it's tough to find true enjoyment with learning. The pitfall to this is that once you graduate, you will be tempted to take off your learning hat for good. Don't! There is always more to learn, and with that knowledge comes a sense of wisdom and fulfillment greater than you can imagine. Life-long learners transcend all barriers - age, gender, race, religion, economic status - and have a sharpness and vitality about them that you won't encounter anywhere else. Have you ever met an elderly person that fits this description? Wouldn't you love to be like her or him when you're that age? The answer is easy to come by. Make an effort to learn something new every day for the rest of your life.

100.

IT'S A BIG WORLD OUT THERE -
HAVE FUN AND MAKE A DIFFERENCE!

Well, we've reached the end of the book! From my perspective, it contains a lot of common sense, some things you've heard a thousand times said in a slightly different way, and a few ideas that are perhaps brand new to you. The bottom line is that I don't want you to make any mistakes regarding your education that you will regret for the rest of your life. None of us in the professional world do. We need great new employees just like you need a great career. I hope this book will help you get on the right track and stay on the right track during your college career, through the job interview process and into the rest of your life.

Remember, college doesn't have to be a chore. It should be a blast from start to finish - a chance to meet new people, discover new things and learn a lot in the process, all the while preparing for your place in the world of work. If you will take the time on the front end to develop good habits, they will quickly become second nature to you. Then, a few short years from now, when you're in the middle of a career you really enjoy, you'll be able to look back fondly on your college years as some of the best years of your life - years well spent!

Last, but certainly not least, remember that our world needs you. Your adult life will see the coming together of our global village in ways not even imaginable a few short years ago. All any of us should wish for is to make a positive difference while we're here. It's your turn! I wish you all the best.

About the Author

Stephen Young is an engineering graduate of Mississippi State University and a former local and national recruiter for Arthur Andersen & Company. He is now a division president for a database marketing/services company in Nashville, Tennessee.

He and his wife, Debi, enjoy music, the outdoors, working with youth, and spending time with their three dogs.

A NOTE TO OUR READERS:

Your feedback is welcomed. Please send your comments and suggestions to the author, care of:

Paragon Press
208 Granger View Circle
Franklin, TN 37064